Leader Lessons

From Invisible to Impactful

By

Diane C. Gaa

Leader Lessons

All Rights Reserved

© 2025 by Diane C. Gaa

This is a work of nonfiction. Names and identifying details of certain individuals have been changed to protect privacy.

Library of Congress Control Number: Applied For
ISBN (Paperback): 978-1-969319-12-9

Printed in the Published
by
Book Writing League (CA-USA)
Support@bookwritingleague.com
www.bookwritingleague.com

Dedication

To every team I have had the privilege to work with and lead, thank you. You gave me your trust, your energy, and your commitment. In return, you taught me more than you will ever know. In your challenges, I found clarity. In your honesty, I found direction. In your commitment, I found purpose. The lessons on these pages are not just mine; they are ours.

To Cindy and Michelle—thank you for not letting me off the hook. You pushed me to get these lessons out of my head and onto paper, and without you, this book would not exist.

And to the leaders who shaped me—your fingerprints are all over the way I lead today.

And finally, to you—the reader—my hope is that these stories make you stop, think, and realize that leadership is not about being perfect. It is about showing up and making it count.

Foreword

When I first became a leader, I thought I had to have all the answers. I thought leadership was about being strong, right, and in control.

I was wrong.

Over the years, I have learned that real leadership is about showing up with honesty, staying curious, and putting people first, even when it is hard. Especially when it is hard.

This book is a collection of lessons I have learned through experience, sometimes painful, always real. Lessons shaped by the teams I have led and those who led me, and the trust we have built along the way.

It is not a guide or a checklist. It is a reflection. A way to look back, take stock, and hopefully offer something useful for others on their own path.

If you have ever questioned yourself as a leader, you are in good company. You are not alone.

Diane C. Gaa

Table of Contents

Introduction

Leadership is one of the most misunderstood roles in professional life. People often assume it is about control, authority, or being the loudest voice in the room. But real leadership, the kind that truly transforms individuals and organizations, begins with a deep belief in your **self-worth.** It is forged through self-awareness, strengthened by overcoming failures, and refined through empathy and thoughtful reflection.

Throughout their careers, leaders take on a range of personas and approaches. Some are undeniably positive, while others can seriously damage relationships and even tear apart a team. Understanding that leaders embody aspects of these various personas is crucial, as is recognizing the immense importance of learning from past experiences.

My own leadership journey has been no exception. For years, I actively shied away from leadership, preferring the safety of invisibility. It seemed like the best defense against adversity and insecurity. However, as my career advanced, I came to realize that the very challenges I had tried so hard to conceal were, in fact, invaluable in shaping me into a leader. My journey, from remaining unseen to making a genuine difference, was far from smooth. It involved a complex, often arduous process of growth that constantly pushed me to adapt and change.

Over time, I realized leadership is not about having it all figured out, it is about staying open to learning from the lessons that come from stumbling, stretching, and sometimes flat-out failing. Each of those moments, as uncomfortable as they were, shaped me into someone stronger and more self-aware. They reminded me that influence comes not from perfection but from persistence, authenticity, and the courage to keep showing up. And with that perspective, I have come to a place where I can confidently say: I consider myself a great leader.

Sounds pretty presumptuous, right? It was not always that way and still today I find myself doubting if I am doing the right thing most days. How do we even define what "good" or "great" looks like? Honestly, it is something we cannot truly know at the moment. A great leader, one that is truly impactful, often will not fully grasp their impact until their teams have moved on, and they can reflect on the profound influence they have had on their careers and lives. Of course, you can see signs from week to week. That incredible feeling you get when you are with your team, a smile or giggle when you notice them mirroring your words or actions, or the immense pride you feel when your team delivers fantastic work, earns an award, or simply does what is right. These are all indicators, helping you gauge if you are on the right path. A leader is not defined by their day-to-day activities, but by the lasting impact they create throughout their career on the individuals within their team.

I still stay in touch with several of my former teammates, and I, even to this date, am genuinely taken aback by the enduring respect shown, several years past their moving on, by the simple words "Thanks, Boss." That might not mean as much to you, but for me, it nearly brought me to tears, because I understand the deep meaning of the word "boss" to those teammates. It is a term of respect and honor, and I am incredibly thankful to be associated with such reverence.

Moments like that remind me that leadership is not about perfection, it is about the imprint you leave on people long after the work is done. That respect was earned not through ease, but through the difficult lessons, the failures, and the relentless effort it took to grow into the kind of leader they trusted and deserved.

My leadership path has been fraught with struggles, and yours will be too. If leading a team feels easy, you are not pushing yourself enough. Every day, I choose to lead with **compassion** and **empathy,** leaving my ego and personal ambitions at the door (or virtual door, these days, with hybrid and remote work). In today's workplace, leading is not about simply showing up at the office, approving a timesheet, or onboarding a new hire. It is about being present.

Over the past few years, I have collaborated remotely with team members stationed around the world. Try leading a team across three to five different time zones, four countries: it is certainly not for the faint of heart. As I mentioned, I commit each day to doing better than the day before, to consistently put my team first and always strive to do the right

2

thing. What **is** the right thing? It is often not easy to determine, as our commitments often involve juggling demands between ourselves, the team, and the organization. Learning to effectively prioritize your team while navigating these competing tasks is a critical lesson you will gain as a leader.

The truth is, finding that balance can feel brutal at times. You will second-guess yourself, disappoint people, and carry the weight of choices that do not have a clean answer. I have been there—and it is in those uncomfortable, pressure-filled moments that real leadership is discovered.

In this book, we will reflect on my firsthand experiences and those of other leaders I observed over the years. Leaders are human; we all make mistakes. How we learn from and apply these mistakes and failures to future experiences is what truly differentiates good leaders from, well, let us just say "those with many opportunities to improve." See how I reframed a negative into a positive? These are just a few of the insights you will gain as you continue to read this book.

This book is a culmination of those moments, real, sometimes painful, but always instructive. I hope these stories resonate with you, whether you are an aspiring leader, a seasoned executive, or simply someone trying to find your voice in this ever-changing world. Leadership is not just a title. It is an attitude, a series of conscious choices, and most importantly, a legacy you leave behind.

Chapter 1
Being Invisible

A leader is not simply born; there is not a single course or book you can complete to magically become one. So, if you were hoping this book—or any course would turn you into a great leader, I'll apologize now. It would be nice if it worked that way, like waving a wand and instantly becoming the kind of leader people look up to. But that is not how it happens. The reality is, you either step up and lead, or you choose to follow. It really is that simple.

For good portion of my early life, I was a follower, observing others I believed held the secret to success. These leaders always seemed to have figured it out. They looked at the part, said all the right things, and on the surface, appeared to be the epitome of leadership. We all carry an image of what a leader looks like, and depending on your generation or life experiences, that image can vary greatly. What does a leader look like to you? Do you see yourself role-modeling others? Are you role-modeling good leader behaviors - or those behaviors that we will highlight in this book as "opportunities to improve"? That is not a throwaway question. It is one I have had to sit with myself, because so much of what we consider "good" leadership is shaped by the messages we absorb early on.

For instance, I was advised to "dress for success." At face value, that sounded simple. But what it really means how to dress, how to walk, how to speak—depended entirely on the people around me and their definitions of success.

I was not sure what success truly entailed. And here is the connection: if we do not take time to define it for ourselves, we risk passing down confused, conflicting, or even harmful versions of what "success" and "leadership" look like to those we lead. Leaders who have not done that reflective work often model behaviors that send mixed signals, sometimes inspiring, but just as often becoming those with "opportunities to improve."

Unsure of what to do, I mimicked various leaders with distinctive styles, some less effective, others truly inspiring. Yet the more I tried to fit into these borrowed molds, the more I realized a difficult truth: leadership is not about appearance at all. Outward polish may capture attention, but it cannot earn respect or sustain trust. What truly defines a leader is not the image they project, or words said, but the substance of their actions and the authenticity of their character. I learned along the way that things are rarely as they appear, and it is in those moments of clarity that true leadership reveals itself. What becomes clear is that leadership is not defined by appearances or titles, but by something deeper.

It is about what people will say about you when you are not around. Take a moment to reflect: how many lives have you impacted? As you consider this, were those impacts positive or negative? And how do you truly know?

I continued to look up to leaders who "looked the part," genuinely wanting to emulate them. I am not entirely sure why I was so infatuated, on the surface, they had it all together, and frankly, they held the jobs everyone coveted. I noticed that while their speech was polished, every word perfect, and their attire impeccable, adorned with the latest designer outfits and not a hair out of place, something was missing. I could not pinpoint it. I only knew what success looked like on the surface. As I got to know these leaders, my illusion of success began to fade. Hearing their teams speaking negatively behind their backs, expressing how they felt untrusted to perform the work for which they were hired. As I mentioned, things are not always as they appear. It was crushing for me to have my image of good leadership shattered, forcing me back to square one. That return to "square one" did more than challenge how I viewed leaders, it pushed me to confront the roots of my own self-doubt.

They say your environment and the people around you shape you. If that were entirely my truth, I suppose I would not be here authoring this book about leadership. My early years were marked by feelings of inadequacy, pervasive self-doubt, and a constant effort to remain invisible. While I could blame it on being the middle of four children, that would not be the honest truth. Perhaps it was because I was bullied for the majority of my childhood, even defensively walking home from school, dodging punches or firecrackers thrown near my feet as I passed the bus stop. I never understood why I was singled out and bullied in that way. For years, I simply believed something was wrong with me. I constantly doubted myself, convinced that someone else always had better ideas, knew better.

I was a follower. Yet, in my gut, I did not want to be one, because I often sensed others were not doing the right thing. Many times, I chose to stay home, invisible, to avoid situations I did not want to be part of, more or less hiding from life. My self-doubt stemmed from allowing it to persist. I never measured up. I did not have anything important to say. I figured others knew more than me, were smarter than me, had better clothes, more money, you can imagine. I bet you can, because like me, you are saying to yourself, "Ah, yep, that's me growing up." If not, you see yourself in the bullies believing that imposing your ideas or will on others was leadership, because that is what you thought it was supposed to look like. The truth is that leadership was never about control. It is about trust, influence, and giving others the room to step into their own strengths. You might be wondering why I am discussing my childhood in a leadership book. Well, I asked myself the same question when I began writing this. Even now, I waited for my dear colleagues and friends to insist I author a book on all the things I have learned before I took any action to actually do it. They would ask, "You have all this insight, why aren't you sharing it?" My answer was, "I don't know." I still have my doubts about whether I will finish this book, or will it ever be published, and even if it is, that anyone would buy it, right? That negative narrative played like a video on repeat, continuously looping, just reinforcing my self-doubt and questioning my abilities. This struggle of negativity and trying not to fall back into invisibility is a day-to-day challenge - and still continues to be a struggle to this day.

So, why was I doubting myself? As I mentioned, I tried to be invisible. I had invisibility down to an artform. Some of it was self-preservation, hiding from the bullies who always were waiting for me somewhere, the snickers behind me in the classroom or the practical jokes kids played that someone thought were funny. Even now in a work environment, those that cannot resist being the center of attention, tearing others down to make others look at them. For the person experiencing these childish acts, it is traumatic. I could blame it all on that, and for many years, I did. "I can't do that; I'm not". You fill in the blanks. We all think about it. The term now used is impostor syndrome.

What I learned in my years of trying to be invisible is that it is impossible. Someone always sees you and will eventually tell you that being invisible is simply wasting your time and potential. It feels safe, but only when you take a chance, choose to be seen, can you truly embrace others and lead. The truth is, staying invisible might feel comfortable, but it limits both you and the people who could benefit from your presence. Leadership is not about being flawless; it is about showing up, letting yourself be seen, and allowing others to connect with the real you. And when you step into that space of visibility, you not only discover your own strength but also begin to notice the hidden potential in others. When you find people with potential who do not feel like they are enough, but you see brilliance in them, when you bring out that brilliance and they see their life reimagined, *that* is leading.

My first role leading a team came about because one person believed in my ability. In the interview, I told the hiring manager, "I can do this job, and if I don't do well, to fire me in six months." I had no prior experience leading teams, no idea what I was getting myself into. No back-up plan. But I did have a willingness to learn, to be a role model, and to always prioritize my team. Because at the end of the day, experience alone is not what defines leadership. What matters most is the ability to put your team first. Every time. No excuses. It does not matter how much experience you have, if you are not putting your team first, you will inevitably fail. That truth has followed me through every role I have held and every leadership challenge I have faced. Leadership is not about proving how much you know, or how long you have been doing the work, it's about whether the people around you feel seen, supported, and prioritized.

That is why I have always found the interview question "Who made the most impact on your career?" difficult to answer. It suggests that a single person should stand out above all others, when in reality, the greatest impact has come from the teams I've been a part of, the mentors who challenged me, and even the colleagues who tested my patience and forced me to grow. It is everyone and every experience.

Each person and experience have shaped the decisions I make, how I feel about myself, my role as a leader, and even the small things like how I show up, my external appearance, do I dress formally or casually, and what those signals to others? Every interaction both good and bad, all contribute to how I am perceived. And when I finally recognized that truth, I began to see a pattern: it was not the big moments or titles that defined me, but the accumulation of small experiences, each one shaping how others experienced me as a leader. These experiences, over time, helped me shift from being invisible into present and visible. That shift did not happen overnight, it happened through intentional choices, repeated daily.

I once knew a manager who constantly strived for perfection. This relentless pursuit of perfection fostered an environment of "fear of failure." What if we made a mistake? Would we be fired? Or worse, would we be singled out in front of our peers? This kind of environment kept me from being visible. Each day, I went to work stressed about making a mistake or the wrong decision. My stomach was in knots. It did not matter that I was good at my job - only that if I made that one mistake - that's what was highlighted. Never the countless times I excelled. Who wants to work in that kind of environment?

Now, you might think, "Oh wow, that person probably isn't someone who had the most impact on your career, right?" Actually, that manager had a significant impact on how I lead today. It taught me to have compassion and empathy when mistakes are made, and while we absolutely want to learn from them, we never want them to negatively change our culture. Mistakes are part of the learning process. Focusing only on mistakes will only foster a culture of fear and you will lose good talent as a result of this. While he definitely had opportunities to improve the fear culture he built, he also opened doors for my career that enabled me to begin my leadership journey.

Lesson 1: *Do not assume that by simply mimicking the behavior of a "good" leader, you will learn everything there is to lead.*

By reflecting on even those negative experiences, you can gain a much clearer understanding of how you want to choose to lead.

Lesson 2: *You cannot lead if you are invisible.*

A good leader must be **visible, vulnerable, and present**. Sharing your story, even when it is uncomfortable, is essential for building trust with your team.

We carry both good and bad experiences with us. They affect how we relate to others, how we make decisions, and, honestly, whether we even want to lead. It is your choice and your obligation to reflect on those experiences and decide if you want to be visible, vulnerable, and present. Are you willing to do the challenging work, even if it is uncomfortable?

Take a minute to reflect on the leaders you have known, those who were genuinely good, and those where there was, let's just say, an opportunity to do better.

What did you learn from them?

- What behaviors do you want to portray while leading your team?
- What behaviors should you be aware of that might negatively impact the team culture you are building?
- How does your behavior impact your brand? How do you want to be perceived?

Reflecting on these experiences will help shape the leader you will become. If you have seen yourself in this chapter, keep reading as we look at how an invisible leader became visible.

Chapter 2:
Becoming Visible

Becoming visible after years of mastering the art of invisibility is like a weight coming off you. I imagine it is like Harry Potter taking off his invisibility cloak for the first time. We all have something that represents an invisibility cloak. It protects us from being vulnerable and exposed.

It could show up as:

- Not contributing to meetings.
- Being afraid to socialize outside of your circle of family or close friends.
- Secluding yourself.
- Not letting others see the "real" you.
- Avoiding travel or social work events.
- Feeling like you need to work long hours to compensate or prove your worth.
- Always trying to prove to yourself and others you are good enough.

While this behavior, in the short term, may feel like a comfortable blanket on a chilly day, becoming visible is essential for others to celebrate all you have to offer. Visibility means to be seen, **really seen**. No hiding places, fully open to judgement by others constructive or not. Without worrying about what others think or do, but leaning into what is right, trusting yourself, and being accountable for your decisions - owning it.

Part of becoming visible is learning to be vulnerable.

Vulnerability is the quality or state of being open to emotional exposure, uncertainty, or risk. It involves allowing others to see your authentic self, including your emotions, weaknesses, and imperfections, often in situations where the outcome is uncertain or where there is a potential for emotional harm.

Vulnerability starts with taking time to reflect on your past behaviors, reconciling the positive and where there are opportunities to improve. It is not something that happens overnight. It requires you to fully embrace your failures and successes. Being fully present, actively listening to your team while showing a side of you that is raw, unscripted, and real. This is the most impactful thing a leader can express. Here are a few things that can help you reflect if you are vulnerable:

- Have you shared past failures with your team? Or were you too embarrassed?
- Does your team know you as a person or just the persona you portray while at work?

These questions are not theoretical for me; they are rooted in my own experience. My years of feeling inadequate, not good enough, continued well into my adult life. Yes, I had friends, earned good grades, and even sang in the high school choir, but I always felt like I was less than. Each time I gained confidence, my internal dialogue kept saying, "You don't have a college degree," "These people are experts, what do you have to contribute?" This messaging of inadequacies replays over and over in my brain. No one wants to feel inadequate. How do you stop it? You don't. The more you fight off feeling inadequate, the more inadequate you will feel. Continuing on this path of self-deprecation only leads to a continued feeling of inadequacy and prevents you from reaching your full potential as a human or as a professional.

It is about changing your perception of yourself from negative to positive. Creating a new message for your brain, a positive message that gives your confidence back, your power to be vulnerable. You do not stop it by pretending it is not there, but by recognizing it for what it is: a story you have been telling yourself. When those thoughts show up, instead of pushing them away, acknowledge them "I hear you, but you're not the whole truth." The goal is not to erase the feeling of inadequacy but to lessen its grip. That happens when you face it with honesty, give yourself permission to be human, and keep showing up anyway. Accept what you cannot control and focus on what you can. Building your confidence helps you step out of the shadows of invisibility. When you begin to trust yourself, you stop hiding behind the version of you that feels "safe" and start showing up as the real you. That kind of confidence does not erase vulnerability; it makes room for it. It gives you the courage to be seen, flaws and all. That level of self-acceptance drives confidence.

Confidence is the belief in one's own abilities, qualities, or judgment. It reflects a sense of self-assurance that comes from internal acknowledgment of competence or preparation, rather than reliance on external validation.

I have seen many leaders or those aspiring to lack confidence for one reason or another. Being invisible usually is the effect of lack of personal or professional confidence. You can be personally confident but lack confidence in a professional setting - or it is both. Maybe like me you lacked confidence in your personal life, and it spilled over into your professional life.

Mid-career, I worked part-time focusing on my family - my boys needed their mom - so my career took a back seat for a while. During that time, focusing on my family, I had more time to devote to their school and opportunities to volunteer. The current Boosters President stepped down - her kids graduated from middle school, and no one stepped up to take on the position. The principal was going to have to make the decision to disband this group if a volunteer to lead did not step up. The Boosters provided significant funding for the school, supported the athletic teams with uniforms and equipment and oversaw running concessions at all home games. At first, I thought - that is a huge job - I stepped back from my career to have time with my boys - I cannot do this - I am not qualified. Again, my self-doubt almost led me to "just leave it be" and let someone else manage it. While I was internally messaging "I can't do this" in my head, my mouth was saying - if no one else will do it "I will."

I was terrified - I never lead a team much less a group of volunteer parents. What was I thinking? Who was I to think I could take this over and do it well? Again, this play was on repeat in my head - over and over. Well, I did it. Not sure how - but I influenced my fellow parents to join me, learning the ropes and I am sure stumbling along the way.

I had to get in front of the parents of all the kids that were playing sports and share what I was planning to do. To this date, I do not remember what I said - I was terrified - it was definitely an out-of-body experience. Words came out - and I got through it.

Fast forward a few years, this stepping up - actually helped me grow into a leader, but more importantly - showed my boys a true lesson. Giving back to others - even when you may not understand what you have to give - is a life lesson to role model. Ten years later, I was the one who was handing over the reins to another parent - one that worked side by side with me and took the group to new heights. Without that spurt of confidence to take this on—at a time when I felt anyone else would be better—the opportunity might have passed. Instead, it opened the door for a successor to continue supporting the school long after my children and I had moved on. That is the paradox of confidence: when you lack it, you not only hold yourself back but also risk limiting the legacy you leave behind.

Lack of confidence holds you back from your potential. It creates a mask and inhibits your aspirations and as a leader keeps you from being vulnerable. That is why building confidence is not just about you. It directly impacts how you show up for your team. When you stand firm in who you are, you are able to set clear expectations, hold people accountable, and support their growth without hesitation.

I always have a plan for each person on my team. Part of that vision or plan is an expectation to ramp up performance year over year. That means if you were performing in one year, the following year expectation required a higher level of delivery. I have been upfront with my team about this expectation and why it is important. Your team wants you to set clear expectations, follow through when expectations are not met, and recognize when they are. This is how you help develop your team to meet your current needs while still looking at what is ahead for them. But development is not only about skills and performance metrics. It is also about building confidence. Without it, even talented people can struggle to deliver at their best.

A teammate was lacking confidence and this showed up as missing deadlines, forgetting about tasks to be done, and a lack of communication and action. Normally, a leader will chalk this up to their need for new skills or taking no action and avoiding the perception of conflict. A leader who is not in tune with their team may call them underperforming and not give the time and energy to really understand the root issue. For this colleague, the solution was not improving skills, it was building up their confidence to perform - give that extra attention and support like saying "you got this." This matters because when people lack confidence, they second-guess themselves, hesitate to take risks, and often play smaller than their true potential. As a leader, if you mistake this for something other than confidence inadequacies, you risk losing out on the very strengths that person could bring to the team. Confidence is the foundation that allows skills to shine. Without it, the best training or tools will not stick. By noticing and nurturing confidence, you are not just helping someone perform better at the moment, you are unlocking their ability to grow, contribute, and lead in the future. When was the last time you provided constructive feedback with empathy?

- Have you set clear expectations not only for performance but continuous learning and development with your team?
- Can you remember the last time you were vulnerable with your team? What experience did you share?
- Do you prioritize your team's performance over your own career aspirations?
- Do you boost the confidence of your team or are you why they are not confident in themselves?

These questions matter because they force us to pause and reflect on how we truly show up as leaders. Aspiration is not only about climbing higher for us; it is about carrying our teams with us as we grow. It is important for you as a leader to have career aspirations - a goal of where you want to take the team and yourself. This will help you fight off feelings of inadequacies and keep you visible while building confidence within your team.

Do not get me wrong, I do not always do this well and I fail often. My aspirations include my team and their success, and this keeps me focused on my goal of being visible, vulnerable, and empathic while leading the team to our collective success. That focus comes from experience. I know what it feels like to shrink back, to doubt myself, and to question my worth. I remember a teammate saying, "She's back," after witnessing me diving back into invisibility, complacency - then self-correcting, turning myself around to the leader I am, and my team deserves. Those very moments have shaped how I lead each day.

Being invisible, my past experiences, lessons learned - good and bad, enable me to have empathy for others who may also feel inadequate, lacking confidence, and undervaluing their own self-worth, because that was me. That journey through invisibility is exactly what taught me how hard the shift toward visibility really is. It is not a switch you flip; it is a discipline you practice, one that requires patience with yourself and persistence in showing up day after day. Becoming visible did not happen overnight; it takes daily work to believe in myself, the leadership vision for my team, and to remove any negativity from my mind - building my confidence. If you are like me, that is not easy, and there will be days you sink back into invisibility, questioning your every move, and even fall back deeper into behavior that does not help your team excel. That is why it is so important to remember that **leadership does not demand perfection, it demands presence.** A wise friend of mine often reminds me of "progress over perfection." When you question yourself or worry whether you are leading in a productive and empathetic way, it's not weakness, it is awareness. Reflection on your actions is healthy; it means you care. In reality, we will always have days where it is easier to choose to be invisible, the day-to-day grind gets too hard, the pressure builds up, and, like most unhealthy habits, we turn to what is comfortable to us, what we know. If that happens to you, stop, reflect, and take a good look at what you achieved that day. Celebrate the little things with your team.

A few leaders over my career did not make it easy to stay visible. Many would delegate work to myself or a team member but then take credit for the work done posing as if it were theirs. This always tends to backfire when a closer look is given, and it is realized that the work was done by someone else. Do you see yourself in this story? This type of leader's behavior is unethical and can, in an instant, erode trust and morale. It discourages open idea sharing and innovation, especially among team members who fear having their contributions overshadowed or stolen.

As leaders, we set the tone for how safe people feel to bring ideas forward. When you recognize contributions and create space for innovation, you send a clear message that every voice matters. The culture you build is shaped by what you choose to encourage and celebrate. And at the heart of that culture is one truth, your team's success is directly tied to your own.

- How do you promote open sharing of ideas within your team?
- What ways do you recognize the team for being innovative and supporting this type of culture?

Lesson 3: *The Success of your team is your success as a leader.*

Team success is your legacy as a leader. How will you show up? Do these stories resonate with you, or do you see yourself? If you tell me "No" nothing in these stories resonates or is comparable to my experience. Well, keep reading, and really reflect on your past experiences. I bet at least one of these stories will get you to say, "Ah ha".

One of the most common places leaders recognize themselves is in how they make decisions. Decision-making has a way of exposing where we stand as leaders. It reveals our confidence, our blind spots, and even the fears we try to cover up. Sometimes, the struggle is not in knowing the right answer but in trusting ourselves enough to choose.

Leaders may show their invisibility through their inability to make a decision. To find confidence in their decision, they ask for validation from the team before acting. I call this persona "Leading by Committee." There are times when we need the team on board and in favor of our decisions. Collaboration has its place, and strong leaders know when to listen and gather input. But if you are leaning on your team to make the call for you every time, you are not leading, you're hiding. That is invisibility in action.

When leaders avoid decisions, they create confusion and stall progress. The team begins to question who is really steering the ship, and over time, that lack of clarity chips away at trust and momentum. Hard choices may not always be popular, but they provide direction, stability, and confidence for the team. Owning your decisions even when they come with risk or pushback shows your team that you are present, accountable, and willing to stand behind your decisions, your ability to lead. That is what keeps you visible and gains the respect and trust of your team.

Here are a few things to consider figuring out if you've fallen back into invisibility:

- Does your invisibility affect your decisions or ability to make a decision?
- Are you in the right state of mind while making that decision?
- How are your relationships affected when you are indecisive?
- Does your invisibility affect your health?
- Does your team trust you? Will they confide in you?

Lesson 4: *Own your decisions. Encourage buy-in from the team but always be courageous enough to make that final call.*

Part of doing this well comes from establishing trust in your leadership capabilities. When a leader has earned their team's trust, the team can accept even the hardest decisions. They may not like the outcome, but they respect that it was made with their best interests in mind. Trust is not easy to come by it takes years to build it but seconds to lose. A key part of building trust is choosing positive language that fosters optimism.

Positive thinking is the ability to approach situations with a constructive and hopeful mindset, even when faced with challenges. A leader with positive thinking focuses on opportunities rather than obstacles, encourages others through supportive communication, and maintains steady confidence in the team's ability to succeed.

It's when you don't ignore problems but instead approach them with curiosity and the belief that they can be solved. It shifts the team's attention from what's wrong to what's possible, sparking creativity and unlocking new options. When a leader models this mindset, it gives the team permission to explore ideas, take smart risks, and act before problems grow. Optimism, when paired with action, builds resilience; it keeps people moving forward even when the outcome isn't guaranteed. Over time, this mindset fosters a culture where challenges are met with

17

energy rather than hesitation, and where performance is driven by possibility rather than fear.

That's why it's so important to overcome the pull of slipping back into invisibility. Reminding yourself that you are good enough, that you can lead, make decisions, and own your mistakes is critical.

It's a conscious decision each day to think about how you need to show up for your team.

Negative thinking is more than a bad mood; it's a slow leak in a team's energy and potential. It shifts focus away from solutions and possibilities, keeping people stuck on what could go wrong. When this mindset takes hold, creativity shrinks, risk taking disappears, and opportunities are missed because the team is too busy bracing for failure to reach for success.

In a leader, negative thinking can be even more damaging. It seeps into the tone of conversations, the way decisions are made, and the confidence the team feels in their direction. Doubt spreads quickly; one leader's pessimism can make an entire team hesitant to act. Over time, trust erodes both trust in the leader's vision and trust in each other.

Negative thinking also kills momentum. Progress slows because people stop leaning forward and start playing it safe. Instead of asking, "How can we make this work?" the team asks, "What if it doesn't?" And with that shift, initiative fades and performance dips.

The reality is challenges are inevitable but how you think about them shapes how you move through them. A leader who can shift the focus from obstacles to opportunities not only protects team morale, but they also maintain the team culture in a proactive, forward-moving mindset that drives results.

To build trust and buy in, you must be visible. In the workplace of today, that doesn't mean the literal definition of "in-person". It means making time for each teammate, listening to their ideas, most importantly, understanding what they need now and being intuitive to what they will need in the future. That mindset also shapes how you approach challenges. The way you frame a problem often determines how your team responds to it.

This is the hardest thing I've had to do as a leader. Your team will mimic your behaviors. By recognizing when you fall back into old habits (being invisible), and quickly adjusting, your team will see your humanity. It is hard, and I struggle with this every day. Showing up for your team in a positive way will build trust and a culture that promotes positive, can-do attitudes. Negativity can erode a team culture. The good news is small intentional shifts can flip the atmosphere almost immediately. What you say, how you say it, and even how you show up physically sends a message that your team will mirror. Here are some ways that have worked for me, where you can see instant change to positivity:

- Change how you react with your words when confronted with an issue. Take a breath, then respond using positive words like thank you for bringing this to my attention. Let's work together on a solution.
- "Fix your face!" Your body language will say it all. If you look like the problem is the end of the world, your team will follow in that negative space.

- "Say 'thank you'". We're often quick to correct, but gratitude should be voiced more often than what could be improved.

The same is true with the words and messages you repeat to your team. What you say and how you say it shapes how they think and respond. My teams have heard many sayings, and we call them "isms." An ism is a saying that helps others rectify their behavior by changing their mindset in the moment. One I use quite often is "There are no problems, only opportunities." Think about some sayings you can use with your team that will instantly make an impact, write them down, and when the issue arises again, repeat them over and over until they stick. Repetition will help you and your team believe in what you say. A consistent and positive approach will help your team feel they are being led in a way that makes them feel safe and that leads to trust.

Immediately, you'll see the tone shift from negative to positive. Being positive in your choice of words, facial expressions, and body language will turn a situation from a gripe session into finding productive solutions. Believe me, it's hard. Each day is a conscious choice to focus on the positive. A positive attitude will also enable you to think about your contributions differently, making you more confident to be visible and vulnerable by sharing your ideas and the stories that shaped your thinking. Nobody is perfect. Keep at it, and when you slide back into negative behavior, and you will, here are a few things to work on daily.

- Start the day with a positive headspace. For me it's a prayer, but for others, it could be just a quiet moment before jumping into meetings.
- Avoid the noise, negative chatter, or gossiping. Everyone will have something to say about everything. Feedback is good, however feedback that isn't constructive and doesn't provide a way forward is noise. Walk away or politely change the subject to something more productive.
- Use words that resonate positivity, i.e., "opportunities instead of problems". Create your own "isms" with your team that helps you communicate with your team keeping conversations positive and focused.
- Give yourself a break, you will fall short, acknowledge it, but keep moving forward. Failure to be positive all the time is inevitable. We are human. Try again the next day and apologize to your team for being too negative. They will appreciate your vulnerability and accept when you are wrong.
- If you make a mistake, apologize and own it. This is extremely important to accept when you are wrong and never blame your team.

These daily practices aren't about chasing perfection, they're about showing up with consistency and building habits that stick. The way you show up sets the tone for your team. When you model these behaviors, you give others permission to do the same. They make visibility possible, create space for trust, and prepare you to lead with empathy.

Lesson 5: *Be visible and lead with compassion and empathy*.

A key part of being and staying visible and impactful begins with having true compassion for others. Compassion is more than feeling sympathy; it's recognizing someone's struggle, understanding their perspective, and caring enough to act. For a leader, compassion shows up in how you listen, how you respond, and how you create space for people to be human without fear of judgment. It's the willingness to slow down, ask the extra question, and offer support that goes beyond a quick fix. This could be an action, or it will be lending a judgement-free listening ear. It definitely isn't about trying to get the last word in or cutting off someone speaking their mind. Always listen and give plenty of time and space - even when your schedule doesn't allow for it.

As leaders, we all have opportunities to build close relationships with our teams. And let's be honest, life doesn't neatly separate itself into personal and professional. Our teams, and even we as leaders, walk into work each day carrying invisible weights, family challenges, health concerns, financial stress, or simply the quiet ache of things not going the way we thought they would.

That's why compassion matters so much. It's not a soft or surface level nicety; it's a leadership strength. Compassion is the ability to lean in with genuine care, to recognize that while you may not fully understand what someone else is going through, you're willing to be present with them in it. Sometimes that means listening without rushing to fix. Sometimes it means giving space without pulling away. And often, it means acknowledging the humanity in front of you, reminding your team that they are seen, heard, and valued beyond the work they produce.

When we lead this way, something powerful happens. Compassion builds trust. **And trust is the currency of leadership.** When people know you view them as more than just their role or their output, they relax into honesty. They feel respected enough to voice what's really happening, safe enough to share when they're struggling, and confident enough to bring forward their ideas without fear. That kind of openness doesn't just strengthen relationships, it accelerates solutions. Problems are surfaced earlier, collaboration happens faster, and the entire team becomes more resilient.

Compassion doesn't mean lowering standards or avoiding hard truths, it means delivering them with care. It's holding people accountable while making it clear you're on their side. It's the balance of empathy and expectation that lets people know you believe in their potential, even when they're struggling.

When compassion becomes part of a team's culture, it changes the way people show up for each other. It creates an environment where resilience grows, where collaboration deepens, and where performance is fueled not just by skill, but by mutual respect and care. To see a team that genuinely cares for each other, supports the work, but also supports each other on a human level is a truly special thing to witness. But that kind of culture doesn't just happen on its own. It grows when leaders model it openly and consistently. Compassion in leadership isn't just a quiet belief you hold. It has to be something your team can see, hear, and feel. That's where being visible comes in. Visibility means you're present in more than just the formal moments. You show up when the pressure is high, when someone is struggling, or when the path forward isn't clear. You don't disappear into your office or hide behind emails when things get hard. You show them you're there and available to them. This may be sitting next to your team in the office, making it known to your team they can reach out and you'll find time for them no matter what is going on in your schedule, or to just be a good listener when they need to vent without fixing the problem or providing judgement.

When leaders are visible, compassion becomes tangible. It's in the way you pause to ask how someone's really doing and listen to the answer. **Really listen**. It's in the time you take to understand the story behind a missed deadline or a dip in performance before rushing to judgment. It's in the small acts checking in after a tough meeting, celebrating personal wins, or offering encouragement before a big challenge.

Visibility builds trust because it shows your compassion is real and lived out through action. Your team sees that you're willing to stand alongside them in both the wins and the struggles. They know you'll show up when they need you most, not just when it's convenient. That presence creates a sense of safety and belonging, making it easier for people to be honest, take risks, and push themselves further because they know their leader is right there with them. And that's the heart of leadership: being visible, being consistent, and being human. Your team doesn't expect perfection, but they do expect you to show up. When you do, you give them permission to do the same and together, that's where growth and trust are built.

Lesson 6: *Leadership isn't about being perfect, it's about being present.*

When you show up with visibility and compassion, you create the trust your team needs to thrive. Trust is the key to team success enabling you as a leader to be impactful to lead with purpose, empowering your team to make a difference. But here's the truth: while trust fuels team success, the definition of success itself doesn't come from the outside world.

Chapter 3:
Definition of Success

Success is deeply personal. It's determined by the values you hold, the integrity with which you lead, and the difference you not only know you're making, but seeing it in action. Others do not determine success; you only determine it.

My definition of success includes my family being healthy and happy, my boys being independent and living their best lives, and for me to do what I was born to do: lead. The saying about doing what you love, and you'll never work a day in your life is so true. If you're a leader because someone tells you that you are, but you aren't passionate or feel this is your calling, don't do it. Leaders love people; they love to help people, lift them up, and help them achieve their goals, even when those goals take them beyond the leader's own team. And that's where one of the hardest parts of leadership comes in, letting people go. Leaders may want to hoard teammates, not wanting to celebrate or recognize their talent for fear of losing them, being poached by others in the company, or worse, another organization. It is our responsibility to develop our teams. When you do this well, you can expect your team members will eventually leave you and that's okay. In fact, it's part of your legacy. Their growth is evidence of your impact. It's the living proof that the time, energy, and belief you invested in others mattered. Their progress reflects your influence, and their success carries your fingerprints.

You know you've led well when your team doesn't just manage without you, they shine. Real leadership isn't about being the center; it's about building others up so that when you step back, their strength speaks for itself. That's the legacy we leave, not in our presence, but in what happens when we're no longer in the room or when our team moves on. And part of building that legacy is seeing the future for our people before they see it for themselves.

As I shared earlier, each person on every team I've led has a future career vision that I see for them. Many times, my team doesn't see it for themselves, or not the same version. If you're a leader and you don't have a vision or plan for each of your team members, you aren't connecting at the level a leader should. I'm not saying you should do exactly what I say, and all will be roses and rainbows. I will say that if you don't have a career direction in mind for each of your team members, your team will fall prey not realizing their full potential or worse left to corporate reorganization, where their skills are considered not in demand. Teams will change over time, evolve, and your team will as well.

What will you do to ensure development of your team is your number one priority? Choose one thing that can make a difference:

- Development discussions regularly
- Co-create a career vision board or plan.
- Co-create performance goals that have a future focus and stretch your teams' capabilities.

These are just a couple of ideas to get you started.

Lesson 7: *Failure to develop for the future is failing your team.*

Success for my team means ensuring every opportunity is available for them to thrive, to develop marketable skills that will transition across a variety of roles and industries. It is about future proofing their existence while using their skills in the present to execute your organization's strategy.

This is a tall order, and many leaders can't even think where to begin first. Don't worry! No one knows the future. However, we do as leaders see signs when change is inevitable, and it's our responsibility as leaders to prepare our team for those changes.

The best thing one of my leaders did for me was to be transparent. The company was going through yet another reorganization. I had survived several in the past, but unfortunately, this one was heading straight toward me. I had an impressive performance record. In that year, I saved the business over a million dollars, but still, the idea of reorganization and redundancy of my role hit me hard. Was it going to be me? I don't want to start over again. Just by the mere speculation of impending change, I was feeling myself sink back into invisibility. The news wasn't official yet - however we all were speculating who would be impacted.

My leader then surprised me. He shared with me the news that my job was in jeopardy and advised me to take an offer to voluntarily leave that came with a nice severance package. I remember the words, "Your role is not in the budget for next year." No one wants to hear those words. I surely didn't. It sounded cruel at the time, but as I reflect on these types of situations as I lead teams over the years, I realize that this action was my leader putting me first. He was bold, did the right thing, and I will always be grateful to him for that.

Unfortunately, one of my peers didn't have as transparent a leader as I did, and her role was selected for redundancy leaving with a smaller, less valuable severance package. I still reflect on that experience and the role transparency played. Both leaders were considered good managers. They supported their teams, invested in development, and, on paper, looked like they were leading well.

But here's the difference: the leader who took the risk to do the right thing—putting his people first was the one remembered. He led with visibility, compassion, and empathy. And because of that, his actions carried weight. They were impactful, not just in the moment, but in the way his team continues to see and remember him.

How do you want your team to remember you when they move on? Will they remember at all? And if they do, will the stories they tell describe a leader who is invisible or one who is truly impactful? The answer to those questions doesn't happen by chance. It comes from the foundation you choose to build every day.

Lesson 8: *Success will only come if you create the foundation to enable it.*

As someone who was promoted into leadership after being known as the one other trusted to deliver - otherwise known as the "Go to person", I had to actively learn to take a step back changing my focus from getting things done to empowering others to be successful.

I was immature in what a leader should do, so I figured, "Let me just pitch in and help the team, I know how to do the job." What I learned is that while I thought I was helping, I'm actually undermining the team. This gives the impression that you don't trust them, they aren't good enough and only perpetuate invisibility within your team resulting in lack of confidence. Any leader who constantly needs to know every aspect of a task or project isn't leading; they're micromanaging. It took me a while to learn this lesson, and it was a difficult road at times. I finally came to the realization, what if someone did that to me? Would I appreciate it, or would I think, "Wow, don't they have better things to do?" or shouldn't they be "leading". After several missteps and a lot of conflict that could have been avoided, I learned that leaders create the vision and strategy, remove barriers, empower, support their development and celebrate the team's successes. Team success makes a leader successful.

It's not about the volume of work you complete; it's about the impact you make to empower your team. Learning this lesson made me realize that if I didn't trust my team to do the work given to them, I would never understand their potential and our potential as a team of what we can accomplish.

I see so many leaders chasing individual success as if it's a quick fix to every problem they face. I call this leader persona "Climbers". Their energy is directed upward, always scanning for the next title, the next promotion, the next chance to be noticed. Along the way, they don't pause to listen or build trust. And if someone gets in their path, they won't hesitate to move past them without apology or looking backwards.

For a while," Climbers" can look like they're winning. On paper, they collect the achievements and accolades that define success. But when you look beneath the surface, the truth shows up in fractured teams, strained relationships, and people who never felt truly valued.

In contrast, there are leader personas I think of as builders. Builders don't measure success by how high they climb, but by how deeply they invest. They show up with compassion, they choose transparency, and they create the kind of trust that allows others to grow. Builders celebrate when someone they've developed takes on a bigger role even if that means leaving their team. Their legacy is not in the titles they've held, but in the people who carry their influence forward.

When I reflect on my own career, I can remember both kinds of leaders clearly. The climbers are remembered for the tension they left behind. The builders are remembered for the way they made people feel seen, supported, and capable of more than they imagined. One fades into frustration; the other lives on in the stories people tell.

I once had to step away from work for several weeks to manage significant personal matters. During that time, I placed my full trust in someone on my team to provide support and keep things moving. I believed in them so much that I even envisioned them as a potential successor to my role. But when I returned, the team felt different. Processes had shifted, and the culture was unsettled. It wasn't a matter of bad intentions—the individual had simply approached leadership in their own way. The real issue was my assumption that trust alone was enough. What I learned is that delegation without guidance can unintentionally set people up to fail. As leaders, we can't just hand over responsibility and hope for the best; we have to equip people with clarity, direction, and support. That experience taught me to be more intentional about developing others and to take ownership when things go sideways. Leadership means building trust, but it also means stewarding it carefully, so the team and the culture remain strong, even in your absence.

So, the question becomes when your team looks back, will they remember you as a climber, or as a builder?

Success, or the drive for success, can be a good thing, but it can also have a negative outcome if individuals are focused only on themselves. If a leader is only thinking about their next promotion, or if a team member only thinks about being the successor to the leader, the focus is on individual aspirations, not the team.

That experience taught me that leadership isn't about trust, it's about what you do with it. Some leaders use trust to climb higher for themselves, while others use it to build something stronger for the team.

The question is: are you a climber or a builder? A builder creates a solid foundation for the team. Like a house, a firm foundation is needed to sustain anything that comes into contact with it or how the foundation can support the myriads of projects and tasks of a team.

The solid foundation for team success includes the following:

1. Be decisive and own it.

2. Set expectations around performance success - and raise these expectations year over year.

3. Build efficiency within your teams, creating time for each other and to learn.

4. Stay in your lane. Empower your team to be the experts, not you.

5. Give space to fail, learn, and apply.

6. Remove barriers that get in the way.

7. Recognize team efforts often.

8. Develop the future workforce and leaders.

9. Communicate with clarity and consistency. People can only succeed when they know where they're headed and why it matters.

10. Model the behavior you expect. Your actions will always speak louder than your words.

11. Lead with empathy and transparency. Trust is built when people feel safe enough to bring their whole selves to work.

Lesson 9: *There is no "I" in "team." There is an E for "everyone."*

Our life experiences inform us of our definition of success. If you cannot think of a leader in your life who positively impacted on your experience, your definition of success will differ from those who have had that positive influence. As I shared earlier, I have been fortunate to have had good leaders and some leaders who had opportunities to improve. Some traits I want to replicate, and others I will discard. Think back to past experiences or jobs, who stood out where there was a leader you looked up to? They may not have been perfect, but something they did or said made an impact on you. That impact influenced how you treat others in your life, whether you lead a team or not. I worked at a large corporation and was a little bored with my current job, so I asked my leader if there were other things I could volunteer to do. Not expecting anything in return, I just wanted to feel like I was contributing to meaningful work as my role had stalled.

Not being engaged with my role, I was excited to sink into new work, even if it meant I had to do it around my current job responsibilities and without any bump in pay. I was placed on a corporate project team whose focus was to create a recognition program for the company. I thought this was a fantastic opportunity to try something new, see how I liked it, and see if I could do the work. At first it was a little foreign to me, but after I met a few new people, got the hang of what was being asked of us, I felt inspired.

I not only loved the work, but it also opened up a new passion for me. We not only created a program but also built the technology to execute it. I was so proud of this accomplishment. I was still doing my current job, which was okay but as I mentioned, not inspiring. It gave a taste of what was possible as a new direction in my career and I didn't know what to do with that. I knew I needed more.

I met with a few people in the company, voiced my interests across the various corporate offices and leaders. This led me to be introduced to a leader in learning and development. She needed some volunteers to help build a course about the company and why we loved working there.

Through this engagement, I met some new people (in roles like mine) but most importantly, learned about the learning and development team and what they were working on. As I listened to what this team did, I thought that was the coolest job ever, and I was committed to seeing how I could help people in that way. Unfortunately, at that time, there weren't any job openings, and I had little experience in learning and development.

So, I kept doing volunteer work while meeting my current job responsibilities, offering my help to others wherever it was needed. Months passed with no new opportunities, but my skills grew, and to my surprise, my left ankle marketability   increased. In the meantime, my network grew, and during that time, a role in that very learning and development team opened up.

I had continued the relationship with the learning and development director even after the project was finished, staying in touch and listening about the amazing projects they were working on. Finally, I heard someone on her team was leaving for a better opportunity. When I shared my interest in joining this team, the leader was thrilled. She was transparent and acknowledged I didn't have all the skills but saw that I was willing to learn. That confidence in me opened not just one door but launched an amazing career helping people improve their skills and changing their mindset to perform higher with confidence.

Had I not developed my skills during that time or taken a chance to change careers, I may not have experienced any of the wonderful opportunities, including those where others trust me to lead them. Development can show up in many ways, it may not always be training, it usually requires a leader to open a door, encouraging us to take the first step towards the unknown with no expectation it will result in success.

On the other side, the leader who took a chance on me discovered something powerful: giving someone an opportunity even if they aren't the perfect fit on paper can create a loyal teammate who's willing to go the extra mile. That trust became the foundation that allowed her to lead with real impact.

And that's the lesson for all of us as leaders. When we take risks on people, when we see potential instead of just checking boxes, we don't just fill a role we ignite loyalty, commitment, and growth. People rise when they feel believed in. They stretch further when someone gives them the space to prove themselves.

Sometimes the greatest impact you'll have as a leader isn't in choosing the perfect candidate, but in seeing what others might overlook and investing in their growth. That's how trust is built, teams are strengthened, and leadership becomes legacy.

Lesson 10: *"Taking a chance on a person may lead to inspiring amazing talent."*

A leader's role is to develop talent. If that leader had passed me by because I didn't have experience in learning and development, I would not be where I am today. I would not have a successful consulting firm, work for amazing organizations, and certainly would not be authoring this book sharing the lessons I've learned throughout my career. That experience shaped how I view success as a leader. It helped me think that I could achieve more for myself, both personally and professionally. Definitions of success aren't one size that fits all. They're influenced by our choices, opportunities, and experiences.

Success, for me, was never about business. As I shared earlier, it was to ensure my sons were raised with love and felt confident enough to do anything they wanted, good to others, always giving back. I am immensely proud of the men they have become as they live their lives learning many of the lessons outlined in this book. This is my greatest accomplishment and my ultimate success.

We are human, we aspire for success both personal and business, and that's okay. Seeking success is a positive thing. It's when you don't have clarity on what success means, you can end up chasing a ghost, something that is always out of reach, leaving you disillusioned and unfulfilled.

So, pause for a moment and ask yourself: *What does success look like for me?* Not for my peers or the voices that tell me what I "should" want, but for me. Because once you define it, you stop chasing someone else's vision and start living your own. That clarity will guide your choices, ground your leadership, and shape the legacy you leave behind.

A team member sent me a post about six traits of a great boss. She said that as she read it, she saw me in the descriptions and thanked me for all I did for them and the team.

It's these moments when you know you're leading in a way that impacts lives. Small quiet successes.

No one expected me to become a leader, actually, the opposite. It wasn't the obvious choice; I wasn't groomed for it and certainly wasn't told I was destined to lead. Maybe your story is different. Maybe you grew up hearing you were born to lead, or you came from a family where leadership was expected because it's all they knew. Or perhaps like me, leadership wasn't something others recognized in you until much later.

Either way, here's the truth: leadership isn't determined by what others expect of you. It's shaped by the choices you make, the character you develop, and the definition of success you decide to claim for yourself. If you don't take time to define it, you risk living under someone else's version of success chasing their expectations while losing sight of your own.

And that brings us to a phrase that gets tossed around often: *"born to lead."* It sounds powerful, even flattering but is it true? Or is it a myth that limits us more than it lifts us? Let's talk about it.

Chapter 4:
Born to lead?

Some people say they were born to lead, but I can't say whether that's true or not. It depends on your definition of success. I know I am a leader because every day I aspire to:

- Put others first, before my own professional success.
- Help others find their true destiny.
- Remember that there is no "I" in a team, leadership is about the "we".
- Lead with genuine care, compassion and empathy for others.
- Shine a light on those who often feel unseen, helping the invisible become visible.

For me, that's leadership. It's not about titles, power, or recognition. It's about serving others in a way that leaves them stronger, more confident, and more capable than before.

And that's the real truth about leadership; it isn't something you're born with or without. It's a daily choice. A choice to rise above yourself, to invest in others, and to lead in a way that leaves a legacy long after the title is gone.

Let's face it, we as leaders aren't perfect, and we don't always exhibit the behaviors we should. Give yourself grace. If you make a mistake today, learn from it and try not to make it tomorrow. Negative rhetoric and mindset only delay your true purpose, your capability to be more than you are today, to strive for more, and for your team. We all make mistakes, it's inevitable. Look beyond what is happening - and "silence the noise." This is when noise gets too loud and you can't focus on your work. I remind the team when this occurs to channel their focus on what's important. Everyone has a perspective, and while some things can be helpful, others are simply "noise." Noise is rhetoric that contributes to the problem without solving or moving us forward. Once you quiet the noise, you can "focus on what you can control" (another ism) to move forward. Many times, I've let the noise defeat me. Keeping me down, stuck in one place. It's funny when I reach that point, it's my team that pulls me out of it. They say, "Focus on what you can control," and those words get me back on track. When I see my team leading me when I'm overwhelmed or not focusing on the right things, that's when I feel successful and know I've made an impact. In that moment, they're not just contributing to the team, they're modeling the behaviors that shape them into the leaders they are becoming.

I didn't have my first team until well into my thirties. I know, I'm a dinosaur, but that's just my story. I spent many years trying to stay invisible, doing what I thought was anything and everything people asked of me, thinking that one day someone would see me. I didn't attend university right after high school. Cash was tight, and honestly, I didn't feel like I could do it. Again, my internal dialogue kept me from pursuing what I wanted in life. I always wanted to be an accountant, after being a singer, of course, but that didn't seem possible with my invisibility cloak on most of the time. A self-proclaimed introvert, I decided to remain invisible for a bit longer. So, I gave up my dream of being an accountant and a singer. I decided to get a job, any job, which didn't involve fast food (hair smelling like grease every day wasn't something I wanted for myself). In high school, we had classes that helped us build real-world skills. I focused on bookkeeping and some computer classes. I didn't realize it at the time, but it was the best decision, minus going to school, because it enabled me to land my first job after high school as an administrative assistant.

Don't worry, I'm getting to the point of being born to lead. Hang in there with me. Many would think I settled, foregoing school, to end up with a job that may not have a career ladder. True, it could have ended up that way, but it was the first chapter of my understanding of the key components of being a leader. An administrative assistant, while the actual title assists a person, also requires initiative, managing schedules, making decisions, managing budgets, and how to eloquently write business emails or letters when you really want to just say, "Do it yourself." I have so much respect for administrative assistants because they are the backbone of the executive team. They lead their executives by making decisions that, let's be honest, the executives are just not able to make. Like most first jobs, you learn from doing the job, but you also learn what doesn't work.

That role taught me something vital: you don't need a corner office or a big title to lead. Leadership shows up in how you take initiative, how you manage responsibility, and how you influence others—even when your name isn't at the top of the org chart. This is where being "born to lead" starts to reveal itself. It's not about pedigree or position, but about determination—the willingness to step in, step up, and keep going, even when the risk of failure is high. And failure will come, but it's in those very moments that true leadership is tested and proven.

That's why I believe leaders aren't born, they're built. Built through failure, resilience, and the choice to keep showing up. Built through adversity. Built through service. Built through choosing, day after day, to lead with empathy, courage, and humility.

I wasn't born to lead—I was made into a leader. And I'm still becoming one every single day.

Every setback sharpens us, every challenge shapes us, and every person we lift up along the way adds to the legacy we leave behind.

Chapter 5:
Following Isn't Leading

As I shared earlier, I wasn't a "leader" until years into my adult life. I always followed the lead of others—following their directions, their vision of what it meant to be a good corporate employee. Even when I didn't agree, I'd convince myself to go along, justifying why it was easier—or safer—to stay the course, even when I knew there was a better way. Don't get me wrong, following the status quo got me noticed as the "get-it-done" person. I built trust because people knew if they handed me something, it would get finished.

But the truth is, I was still looking to others to pave the way. I think this instinct came from years of feeling invisible. That "cloak" of invisibility followed me from childhood into adulthood, and it kept me from having the experiences that forces us to step up—to lead, to fail, and to learn. No one can truly lead while hiding behind an invisibility cloak. It dims their shine before it ever has the chance to show.

Leaders don't disappear when they're needed most. They don't step back from responsibility or leave others to steer without guidance. True leaders remain visible. They set direction, make decisions with clarity, and stay engaged, especially when the path forward feels uncertain. And yes, they also know when to follow—listening, learn, and give space for others to shine. Knowing when to step back is just as much a mark of strong leadership as knowing when to step forward.

The truth is, I had no idea what leadership was supposed to look like. I had a talented team and figured it out over time—mostly through trial and error. With no formal training, I mimicked the leaders I observed around me. Sometimes that worked; sometimes it didn't. Mimicking only helps if the leader you're modeling puts their team first, not themselves.

One of the toughest lessons I learned came during times when I had to conduct layoffs and terminations, as most managers eventually faced. It never gets easier to let someone go, whether it's because they failed to learn from mistakes, or because of a reorganization or company decision. I often ask myself: why does it have to be this way? Isn't there a better way? Sometimes, the answer is no, you have to do the challenging thing. But other times, leadership means standing up for your team and what's right.

In either case, how you show up matters. Being transparent and empathetic in those moments will always earn respect. Empathy means caring enough to understand people, and transparency means being honest enough to keep their trust. Together, they form the foundation of leadership that people will remember long after the decision has been made.

In one situation, I was specifically asked not to give advance notice of the meeting context where we were informing employees about an organizational change. This bothered me, but I didn't listen to my gut and instead I followed orders. I met with the employee and delivered the news as instructed. The employee told me I was misleading and manipulative to ask someone to come to a meeting without a clear understanding of what it was about. I get it, she was right, but I was following orders, as I've done repeatedly. I wasn't leading, I was following. I didn't like myself. After that call, I cried. I was sad about not supporting my team in the way I would want to be supported. I wish I had taken more time to ask questions about what I could legally do, something a little more supportive, where I wouldn't be perceived as someone who didn't care.

I do care. Isn't that what a leader does? They care about their team, about people, and about the work they do.

You'd think I would have learned, and I did, a little, but I still followed orders even when I didn't agree with the outcome. But leadership has a way of putting the choice back in your hands.

This time, there was no one else to hide behind—the decision was mine. I had to trust what I saw, what I felt, and what I believed was best for the team. I interviewed several people for an opening on my team. All were exceptional and equally qualified, but one stood out to me. I was ready to offer them the job when a colleague manager asked me what I was doing. I told him I was hiring the best candidate. Well, my colleague was concerned that the candidate wouldn't be a good fit in the office because the bathrooms wouldn't be accommodating.

I was frustrated with my colleague. Why is this a problem? I just wanted to hire the best person to do the work. Instead of following my gut, I let outside voices influence me. I hesitated, second-guessing myself. Were they right, or was I? I slid back into invisibility, lacking the strength and courage to be decisive and follow my gut. I finally came to my senses and asked my first candidate to join the team. Luckily, they graciously agreed and ended up being a valued and endearing member of the team.

Follow your gut. You know the right thing to do. Don't let others influence you to do the wrong thing. Be bold and stand up for what you believe.

It took me several bad decisions to learn I needed to be a leader, not a follower. Leaders don't naturally lead. Many begin as followers, doing what they're told despite their own beliefs or values. I didn't want the next time to be another failure.

Sometimes we follow because we're afraid, afraid of losing our job, missing promotions, or because we just don't have the confidence to believe that what we think is right. I believe these were the reasons behind some of my choices: I was afraid to lead. After all, it's easier to follow.

Reflect on some times when you may have made a choice you regretted:

- Did you learn from that mistake?
- What would you do differently?

Repeating the mistakes of the past means you didn't learn your lesson. I was weak. I followed and didn't lead. I didn't put my team first. I caved.

I still think of those past lessons even today, years later. I sometimes see some of my teammates on social media, with new jobs, promotions, and recognition, and I'm thankful for that. Thankful that my mistakes didn't impact on their ability to thrive.

A leader can either positively impact someone's life or break their self-worth and ability to believe in themselves enough to get back on their feet.

In today's business world, many leaders are still followers. They do what they're told, even if their gut is screaming no. Why do we keep doing this? Most likely, it's fear.

Follow your gut. That's the saying, so you don't lose your sense of what's right versus wrong. Be strong and make the hard choices. In situations where you can't stand up the way you want to, find out how you can at least make the situation more tolerable, more empathetic.

The golden rule is to "do unto others as you would have them do unto you." Why don't we follow this simple statement? Because it's hard. It takes every ounce of courage to go against the status quo and do the unpopular thing, to go against your boss's wishes or the company's direction, even when you know it's right. I'm not endorsing going against policy or legal requirements. However, if something is fundamentally wrong, why aren't we questioning it more?

A leader stands up for what they believe is right and always considers the needs of the team.

- Follow your gut.
- Follow the "Golden Rule".
- Find ways to do even the hard things in a caring, empathetic, and respectful way.

Will you stand up for what's right? Can you reflect on a situation you'd love to hit replay or get a redo? We all have one or ten! Next time you have a situation where you're being drawn into invisibility, following others' leading you to an outcome that you know is wrong - stop, reflect, and put yourself into your team's shoes. Would you like this outcome to be yours? If not, then choose your team first!

The truth is that leadership isn't about going along when you know the direction is wrong. It's about having the courage to pause, challenge the moment, and choose a better path not for your own comfort, but for your team's future. There are times when following is powerful when it means listening, learning, and giving others the space to lead. But when following pulls you into invisibility or forces you to compromise your values, that's when you must step forward. Real leadership is choosing what's right, even when it's hard, and showing your team that you will always stand with them, where it matters most.

Chapter 6:
Proactive Versus Reactive

Leaders who are followers aren't leaders; they're order takers. I tell my team all the time: we're here to provide a service by anticipating the customers' needs. This doesn't mean doing whatever anyone asks, no matter who they are and how high in the organization they sit. By thinking proactively and focusing on the real problem, they're leading. They take the initiative to proactively address their customers' or stakeholders' needs by doing the demanding work to provide valuable solutions.

Proactivity means staying a step ahead. It's anticipating challenges before they show up at your door, spotting opportunities before they pass you by, and acting before anyone has to nudge you. A proactive leader doesn't wait for problems to pile up or for someone else to make the first move; they prepare the team, put plans in place, and clear roadblocks early so the work can flow.

Being proactive also isn't about doing everything yourself, it's about creating the conditions where your team can thrive without constant fire drills. It's keeping your eyes forward, your mind open, and your actions deliberate, so you're leading the way instead of scrambling to catch up.

However, leading reactively is living in response mode waiting until problems are in full view before addressing them. It's constantly shifting focus to put out fires, juggling urgent issues instead of guiding the team toward long-term goals. Reactive leaders often feel busy, sometimes overwhelmed, but rarely feel ahead, because their time is spent dealing with what's already happening rather than shaping what's next.

Being reactive can drain a team's energy and confidence. People start to brace for the next crisis instead of building for the future. Decisions become rushed, communication gets strained, and opportunities slip by because everyone is too focused on catching up. While every leader will need to react at times, staying in that mode too long keeps the team in survival mode rather than growth. A leader's first responsibility is to empower, and in turn, led by removing the obstacles in the path so they can be successful, perform at their best, and provide the company with a service that enables more customers to be served. Removing obstacles is one of the most important jobs a leader has. It's about scanning the path ahead and noticing what could slow your team down whether it's unclear priorities, a decision that's stuck in limbo, outdated tools, a missing resource, or even an unspoken tension between people. Then, it's acting quickly to address it so your team can focus on doing their best work.

Great leaders don't just react when an obstacle is pointed out, they anticipate what might trip the team up before it becomes a roadblock. Sometimes that means having tough conversations, renegotiating deadlines, or pushing for resources others are hesitant to give. Other times it's as simple as clarifying expectations or connecting the right people at the right time.

Removing obstacles isn't about doing the work for your team, it's about creating the conditions where they can move forward with clarity, confidence, and momentum. When leaders consistently clear the way, the team learns to trust that their energy will be spent on progress, not on fighting through avoidable barriers.

Empowering your team to lead reduces the possibility of them becoming followers in the future, becoming invisible. Empowerment is more than handing someone a task; it's trusting them with the responsibility and authority to own it. It's giving people the tools, resources, and clarity they need, then stepping back enough for them to make decisions and act in their way.

True empowerment starts with trust. You believe in someone's potential before they've fully proven it, and you make it clear that you're there to support them if they hit a roadblock. It's about creating a space where they can take risks, experiment, and grow without the constant shadow of micromanagement.

Empowered teams think for themselves, solve problems faster, and bring forward ideas that would never have surfaced if they were only following orders. They feel valued not just for the work they deliver, but for the perspective and creativity they bring.

For a leader, empowerment requires humility, the willingness to let go of control, to share credit freely, and to allow others to shine. It's knowing that your success is measured not by how much you achieve, but by how capable and confident your team becomes because you believe in them.

When empowerment is genuine, it builds trust, fuels ownership, and creates a team that's stronger than the sum of its parts. And that's when real leadership happens not when you're at the center of everything, but when your people know they have what it takes to lead in their own way.

Lesson 11: *A team that is proactive, is a team that leads.*

A leader's role is to unlock the full potential of their team—because when people are supported and trusted, they naturally deliver at their highest level. It starts with trust believing that each person can take ownership of their work and make decisions that move the team forward. You give them the clarity of purpose, the resources they need, and the freedom to approach challenges in their own way.

When a team feels empowered, performance changes. People stop waiting for instructions and start taking initiative. They anticipate problems, propose solutions, and bring forward ideas that improve outcomes. Work doesn't bottleneck at the leader's desk because decision-making is distributed, allowing the team to move faster and with more confidence.

Empowered teams are also more resilient. Because they have the authority to act and the trust to experiment, they adapt quickly when plans change. They don't freeze in uncertainty; they figure out the next step and take it. This autonomy fuels accountability: when people feel they truly own their work, they hold themselves to higher standards.

For leaders, empowering a team isn't about stepping back entirely; it's about staying connected enough to guide, support, and remove obstacles while resisting the urge to control every move. The result is a team that performs not because they're told to, but because they're invested in the outcome.

When empowerment becomes part of a team's culture, performance isn't just measured in metrics, it's seen in the energy, creativity, and pride the team brings to every goal. That's when you know you've moved from managing tasks to leading a high-performing, self-driven team.

- Do you empower your team to lead?
- How do you help remove obstacles? Or are you in the way?
- What can you do differently next time?

I worked in a large organization and was responsible for delivering training through our learning platform to 40,000 employees. I was young in my leadership career, and it was a big job for anyone at any age. I led a team of incredibly talented professionals across the globe over five time zones, yes, everyone had only a few hours between us to collaborate, and our start and end of our day covered 24 hours. We had to; we supported a large group of people, and if something went wrong, someone needed to be available to help.

We were designing compliance training and were proud of what we created. After asking others for feedback, everyone said it was fantastic and helped them learn the topic. Great, right? The team did what was asked of us, we received some valuable feedback, and all should have been great.

Not so fast.

The first couple of days went fine, with minimal support tickets, just typical bandwidth issues or people not reading the directions. (Why is that? No one reads anymore, oops, wonder if they'll read this book?) Anyhow, back to the story.

About a week after launch, we received a support ticket. Someone couldn't finish the course. I thought, well, they must not have read the instructions, or it's something simple. After troubleshooting and trying to figure out the problem ourselves, we couldn't figure it out. We then asked the person to show us the issue in a virtual meeting.

We found out that, when using a screen reader device, the navigation buttons (that we were so proud of, and thought were gorgeous) were impeding him from completing the course. I was so embarrassed. How could I not verify that it would work with assistive devices?

At the time, I was unaware of what an assistive device was, why someone would need to use one, or how to design our product to accommodate it. But I did know that I needed to lead my team to fix this and fix it fast. I was frustrated that we didn't anticipate the needs of all of our customers.

That was the moment that everything changed.

It was through that frustration that I knew we needed to turn things around, think about others first, with all abilities, to understand how our colleagues would access our content, and to design with inclusive and accessibility in mind. That was the goal, and it was a great goal. Where do I begin, I asked myself. How do I make this happen?

That was the lesson that helped shape the way I knew I should lead. No more following.

I met with my team, and we worked out a plan to learn everything we could about accessibility and accessible design. I was motivated, the team was motivated towards a common purpose, to elevate our solutions; no more being embarrassed, taking control of what we could do. It took about a year for us to learn everything we needed and begin to affect change. Focusing on what we could control, small things that could make a big impact, was our focus. Slowly over time, we all became quite expert in how to bring learning to life that is inclusive and accessible. We were being proactive, anticipating the needs of the colleagues, and through this, the team rallied around a common purpose. Finally, I was beginning to see a change in my confidence as a leader and the team's trust in me to lead them. This was the beginning of my invisibility cloak finally coming off. I was tired of following, it felt good to lead.

The road from being reactive to proactive is hard. Most people wait until there's a problem and then solve it; that's reactive behavior. Reactive behavior is when someone responds after something happens. It's instinctive, unplanned, and usually triggered by an outside event or person. Instead of anticipating what's coming, the person waits for a situation to unfold then scrambles to deal with it. If you lead reactively, your team will always be in reactive mode. That means there's no time to move forward, reach your vision, or execute your strategy. It just can't be done.

Reactive teams often spend the majority of their time, sometimes up to 80 to 90% putting out fires, answering messages, and responding to problems as they come. In contrast, high-performing teams that focus on being proactive aim to flip that ratio, spending most of their time planning ahead, preventing issues, and driving long-term results. The more time a team can shift toward proactive work, the more control, clarity, and impact they gain. Imagine what you could do if that were flipped. What if your team spent only 10 to 20% of their time fixing problems, and the rest innovating, advancing ideas, and developing skills not just for today, but to anticipate future needs?

- Is your team reactive or proactive?
- How much time could be saved for your team if you stopped being reactive?
- What is one thing you can do today to change that?

After I lost my job due to an organizational restructuring, yes, the one my leader warned me about and told me to take the better severance package, I took some time to reflect on everything I'd learned over those 18 years. I realized I could help others, especially with the lessons I'd learned helping my team shift from reactive to proactive.

I had a nice severance package, and in my state, I could also draw state unemployment benefits, so I figured, why not? I'd open a consulting firm and see how many people I could help with the lessons I'd learned over the years.

So, I reached out to several former managers and teammates to let them know I was open for business. I was on my way as an entrepreneur. The problem was, I had all this experience, and no customers. I knew how to lead a team, or at least I felt I did. But this was bigger. Harder. And I kept seeing my self-doubt creep in.

Luckily, one of my former leaders reached out and recommended me for an opportunity with an organization that needed help solving a few problems. As I read the challenges, I knew they were the same ones I'd faced with my team in the past: being reactive, having no time to innovate, a project lists a mile long with no plan to execute.

Sound familiar?

I accepted the challenge, but the team didn't. They were comfortable with how they were working. I had to shake things up, but how do I do that without alienating the team? Good question. I knew I had to trust my gut.

So, I had a long conversation with the team, sharing ideas about how we could become more proactive by anticipating the needs of our customers. Thinking more strategically. It sounded good at the time, but the work involved required everyone's buy-in. Most people agreed. One person decided to leave. Another was skeptical but agreed to try it.

A few years later, that skeptical colleague told me his experience had been that consultants come in with ideas that never pan out, so he was expecting this to fail, too. I got it. I didn't want to waste anyone's time with ineffective approaches either. But I knew this worked because I had seen it work before. Not once, but twice. I felt it was a proven approach.

But I lacked the trust of the team.

Lesson 12: *Trust Is the Foundation for Meaningful Change.*

When people believe in your intentions and your integrity, they're willing to lean into uncertainty and try new ways of doing things. Change by nature requires people to leave what's comfortable and step into what's unfamiliar. Without trust, that step feels risky; with trust, it feels like a shared journey. Trust creates space for honest conversations, mutual respect, and the benefit of the doubt when challenges arise. It's not a "nice to have" it's the currency that buys commitment, resilience, and momentum when leading transformation.

Without trust, I had to quickly show them how their work lives could be positively impacted by the approaches we were applying. Thankfully, the team gave it a shot. Even the skeptical one believed they could do it.

It was a long, hard road; it required us to change our processes and specifically how we design to ensure all issues were found before launch. So, this required re-training the team on what good looks like. We had brilliant designers with years of experience, but their designs were overshadowed by a frustrating experience with content freezing, spelling mistakes, and lack of accessibility. It was not an overnight change. It required diligence by the team to be accountable and not slide back into bad behaviors. Over time, the team was responding to fewer support tickets and was finally able to tackle the long list of backlog projects, the ones that sit untouched when you're always in firefighting mode. The experience was difficult, time-consuming, and required full trust by the team of my ability to lead - not fall back into invisibility - to lead with passion and with empathy.

Trust isn't automatically granted. They might give you a chance, but you have to prove that your leadership will help them be successful.

Fast forward a year after the change: that same skeptical colleague told me he had serious doubts at first and thought, "This is never going to work." But he thanked me for coming in and helping the team. He saw now that the way they'd been working wasn't helping anyone, and he was proud of what we as a team had accomplished.

A few years later, that team member was promoted to another role and is already making an impact using the lessons learned through his lived experiences. The outcome of this change? I had earned the trust of my team, an amazing feat. Together, we reduced support tickets by 60% in the first six months and by 80% within the first year. Even more incredible? We've sustained those results for several years.

What a feat, and a proud moment, only made possible with the trust of the team and a leader that truly led - leading the team to proactive behavior.

When teams are trusted to make decisions and take ownership, they stop waiting for direction and start looking ahead. They scan for challenges before they become roadblocks and spot opportunities before they slip away. Empowered team members don't just react to what's in front of them; they anticipate, prepare, and act early because they feel responsible for the outcome. This forward-leaning mindset turns empowerment from a feel-good concept into a performance driver, creating a team that stays ahead instead of catching up.

Is your team proactive or reactive?

- Do you respond to issues, or are you anticipating the needs of your customers, colleagues?
- Do you have a backlog of projects a mile long or maybe a stack of to-do lists?
- Does your team trust you to effect change? Why not?

A leader without trust is like a leader without a life vest. Trying to stay afloat but slowly the water covers you, suffocating you - you can't lead when you are in survival mode.

How do you gain trust after it's lost? That is a hard question, it's not an overnight fix. Humans trust in most cases unless their past experiences have led them to mistrust. Depending on your team and their lived experiences, it may take longer to build trust if the history has been of disappointment and frustration leading to distrust. It can be done—and the effort is worth it. Rebuilding trust isn't about pretending the cracks were never there; it's about showing that even with the scars, the team can become stronger than before. By choosing to repair relationships with positivity and moving forward with intention, distrust can transform into a deeper, lasting trust. Trust is essential for teams to feel psychologically safe. Without that feeling of safety, it is impossible to lead, you might manage but you won't lead.

Psychological safety means people feel safe to speak up without fear of being judged, punished, or embarrassed. It's the kind of environment where team members can take risks, admit mistakes, ask questions, and share ideas even unpopular ones without worrying about negative consequences.

- How can you help your team feel safe?
- How do you handle failure? How does that show up within the team?
- Do you build trust or erode it?

- What can you do to build trust in your team?
- What will that look like for you? How will that make you and your team feel?

Chapter 7:
When Trust is Lost

When trust is lost, it's rarely the result of one giant mistake. More often, it's the small things that pile up over time—missed follow-ups, shifting priorities without explanation, or a leader who stops listening because they're too focused on their own agenda. Those small cracks widen until one day the team no longer feels safe bringing their full selves forward. I've seen it happen people stop volunteering ideas, stop asking questions, and stop believing their leader has their back. It doesn't look dramatic at first, but the silence speaks volumes.

I remember working on a project where deadlines kept slipping, not because the team wasn't trying, but because leadership wasn't giving clear direction. Instead of owning the confusion, the leader doubled down—pushing harder, demanding results, and blaming the team when things didn't click. Slowly, trust eroded. Team members who were once outspoken went quiet. Collaboration turned into compliance. You could feel the energy drain out of the room. The real damage wasn't in the missed deadlines—it was in the belief that their leader couldn't be counted on.

Rebuilding that kind of trust takes grit and humility. It means a leader has to stop pretending and start owning their part of the problem. In this case, when the leader finally acknowledged, "I failed to give you what you needed, and that's on me," the mood shifted. It didn't erase the past, but it opened the door to healing. Over time, with consistent follow-through, the team began to lean in again. The cracks were still there, but they became reminders of what the team had overcome together.

The point is this: when trust is lost, it doesn't mean the story is over. If anything, it's a chance to write a stronger one—built on honesty, vulnerability, and the determination to prove, day after day, that people can believe in you again.

Instead of letting this lesson change you, use the opportunity to teach what great leadership should look like. Do you remember a time when your team lost trust in you? Or you lost trust in a team member?

- How did you handle it? How did you take accountability?
- What will you do differently next time?

Chapter 8:
Developing Your Team by Building Trust

We have talked a lot about trust underlying as the foundation intermingled in all relationships, those new and those more established. Before you can even think about helping your team develop, you must build trust. So, how do you do that? There are several ways, but in my experience, the best way is to be transparent, honest, and trustworthy. Trust isn't granted automatically; it takes time to build trust with your team. I remember in several of the teams I built over the years, I selected team members purposefully who had a variety of personalities and skills. Each one contributed uniquely to the team. They didn't magically trust me at the start; I had to prove I was worthy of that trust. I had to show them that I could keep their confidence and that I could lead them where they needed to go.

One way I was able to show trust was by being vulnerable. I shared very personal parts of myself, even things I did not share with my own leader. I had to trust that they would keep my confidence, and in turn, I would keep theirs. That was the first step.

- Have you shared an experience with your team that is personal, makes you vulnerable, or uncomfortable?
- Has your team seen you fail? How did you handle failure? Did you cover it up, blame someone? Or were you vulnerable to share this with your team as a learning experience?

It was important to trust that my team would perform well and, in turn, make me look good. Their success is our success.

Some people say being vulnerable isn't a good look for a leader. I say it's the key to finding one. The more vulnerable you can be with your team, the more vulnerable they will be with you, the greater the trust that's built.

It is impossible for an invisible leader to be vulnerable. It's hard to feel exposed, and after many years of invisibility, I was afraid to be vulnerable, afraid that vulnerability meant I wasn't cut out to be a leader.

Being vulnerable means being exposed. By withholding the real parts of yourself your doubts, fears, or emotions you don't feel exposed, a protective move that keeps you safe but also keeps relationships shallow, limits trust and hides the authenticity that builds real connection. For a person who has spent most of their life trying to be hidden or invisible, being in the spotlight telling your story, very personal excerpts about experiences that are important lessons you want to share, exposes you in a way that is frightening, unsettling, and difficult, especially if you lack confidence in yourself. Sometimes experiences are so raw, bringing all your energy to think about them, not even speaking about them, will take time, patience with yourself, and trust in your team. It takes time. None of the lessons in this book are easy, but they are worth it if you take one step, one change, and build upon it. Take time to reflect on a story that you'd like to share with your team but are afraid.

- What value is your team missing because you are not being vulnerable and sharing this experience?
- By sharing it, will it help you reflect, heal, or move forward? Is it holding you back from being visible?

Focusing on your ability to be open and honest with yourself and others will give you the courage to be vulnerable. Without vulnerability, you are unable to properly support your team's development. Sure, you can recommend training, have a conversation about performance; check the box. Being vulnerable enables you to let people see the real you, your hopes, your doubts, your mistakes without trying to control how they'll respond. It's a choice to be open, knowing it invites trust, deepens connection, and creates space for others to do the same. This will enable you to build trust with your team, so that you can begin to have those development discussions that are focused, future-oriented, and impactful.

How does vulnerability or lack of it impact your team?

As I shared earlier, leaders do have to juggle many responsibilities, and yes, some days the work is difficult and sometimes unbearable. A first step to being vulnerable is accepting accountability and failure. A team that knows its leader has their back will always put in extra effort, if for nothing else, out of sheer respect for the leader. Sharing that you made a mistake when you do, or when you don't have all the answers, helps your team understand that you're human, therefore building trust.

Transparency is key to building trust. Transparency means being open and honest about what's happening—sharing information, decisions, and reasoning clearly, even when it's uncomfortable. It's about keeping people in the loop, not in the dark.

People can usually handle tough news. What they can't handle is silence, secrecy, or being blindsided by decisions that affect them. When leaders hold back information or gloss over the truth, the team fills in the gaps on their own. And let's be honest, the stories we create in our heads are often worse than reality. That's why transparency matters—it prevents unnecessary doubt and stops assumptions from taking root.

Being transparent doesn't mean you have to share every single detail or pretend to have answers you don't. It does mean showing respect by letting people know what you can, when you can, and why decisions are being made. Sometimes the most powerful thing a leader can say is, "Here's what I know, here's what I don't, and here's what I'm committed to finding out." That level of honesty builds credibility.

Transparency is also about consistency. It can't be something you practice only when it's convenient. The moment you choose to be open, you risk damaging the very trust you're trying to build. Teams thrive when they know their leader will be upfront with them—whether the news is good, bad, or somewhere in between. That predictability creates stability, and stability fuels trust.

At the end of the day, transparency is more than leadership skills. it's a leadership mindset. It signals to your team: *I trust you enough to tell you the truth, and I respect you enough to include you in it.*

Once you have the trust of your team, it makes conversations around how to ensure you are continuously learning and developing a bit easier. These are key to your team's viability. That doesn't mean you or they will stay in the same role year after year. What did I say about change if you aren't moving? You are standing still. Standing still in business means you are dying, you are not growing, you are stale. As leaders, we must keep our teams developing to not grow stale and build marketable skills that are in demand and sought after. Without trust, it's impossible to have meaningful development conversations.

Lesson 13: *Development conversations are a key part of building relationships with my team.*

I saw some changes in the organization and the lack of opportunity for a team member to go beyond their current role in our team. We had worked hard on building up his skills, both human and technical skills, and felt he was ready to move on. I shared a job opening in the organization that would stretch his skills. At first, he was hesitant after being comfortable in a role for many years and was excellent at it. I had to be transparent, share with him that there wasn't a clear pathway in the learning team for him to progress, at least in the direction of what he loves to do. I explained that I felt this role was a good opportunity to indirectly work with the current team while expanding his skills to grow, which in turn would help him in his career trajectory. That was hard. I didn't want him to leave the team, but I needed to be transparent and put his needs, current and future, first. In this case, he took my advice. Your team will not always follow your career advice. That's okay as I said earlier, your team will create their own path. It's a leader's responsibility to support them, direct them, but also redirect if choices made along the way don't pan out for them. This doesn't stop when they no longer directly report to you. If you apply these lessons, your team's relationships will outlast your tenure in your leadership role.

- Do you put your team's needs before yours?
- Can you think about a time when you were transparent? How did your team react?
- Do you have regular development conversations?
- Do they trust you to have their best interests in mind?

I was leading a team and had an opportunity to expand my team. I had worked with a colleague on another team and knew she was perfect for an opening I had supporting the learning platform. I knew she was perfect, but she wasn't convinced. It meant she had to take a chance at a new role - one different from her current role. Leaving a role where she had seniority and was comfortable with the expectations and her ability to perform. It was a big ask - a scary ask. At first, she was resistant, and I don't blame her. I had a small window of opportunity to fill these openings, so as much as I wanted her to join - I knew she had to trust that there was something bigger, an opportunity that could not be achieved by staying in her current role. Despite having confidence that taking this opportunity was a good idea, I had to show trust that I could support her to learn new skills, ones that would take her further in her career. That's the heart of leadership: recognizing potential and then creating the space for it to grow.

Because development doesn't just happen by chance—it's real, continuous, and intentional. It's the work of becoming more capable, more self-aware, and more ready to take on what's next. It's not just about gaining skills; it's about stepping into more impact, more clarity, and more ownership. True development doesn't happen by accident; it's a choice to keep learning and stretching forward.

The mindset of you and your team plays heavily into this. If your mind is not focused on continuous learning, and your team culture does not support this, your team will stand still. As I shared earlier, a company that stands still will eventually die. A colleague who stands still will also lose their marketability, relevance to the team, and to the organization.

Continuous learning is a mindset it's choosing to stay curious, stay open, and keep growing no matter how much you already know. It's not just about taking courses or reading books; it's about learning from every experience, every piece of feedback, every win, and every misstep. It's the difference between coasting and evolving. In leadership and life, if you're not learning, you're stuck.

And all of this, growth, development, curiosity, and continuous learning come back to trust. Without it, even the best intentions fall flat. Your team won't open up about where they want to grow, won't take the risks needed to stretch, and won't believe you have their best interests at heart.

But when trust is present, everything changes. Development conversations shift from being uncomfortable to empowering. Feedback becomes fuel instead of criticism. And growth both yours and theirs becomes possible because the foundation of trust makes it safe to keep moving forward together.

So how do you build a continuous learning team culture? It begins with you as a leader; you set the tone you lead and set the expectations that it will be.

One way to do this is to include development conversations in your regular 1:1s. What, you don't have regular 1:1s? What is more important than this? Nothing. Regular time with your team not only helps you build trust, but it is essential for you as a leader to coach, share feedback, and lead the team through individual and team growth.

- Do you have a development goal or objective? Have you shared it with your team?
- Does your team have a development goal or objective? Why not?
- How often do you have development conversations? Is it only when performance review time comes around?

For those reading who are doing the right thing, you have regular conversations about development, you are enabling your team to grow and perform higher. So, what's next? I am so glad you asked this. It's time to raise expectations to help stretch the team's ability to go further, higher. Develop through coaching.

Coaching is a partnership that helps people grow by asking the right questions, challenging assumptions, and creating space for reflection and clarity. It's not about giving answers or fixing someone; it's about helping them unlock their thinking, make better decisions, and move forward with confidence. At its core, coaching is about trust, truth, and growth, meeting people where they are, and helping them get where they're meant to go.

- Do you coach your team or just give orders or answer questions?

- Do you focus on your team by listening - or do you monopolize the conversation, focusing on yourself?

Leading means you are coaching your team to develop to their next level. It's asking questions that spark their thinking, giving feedback that builds confidence, and creating space for them to try, learn, and grow. It's less about handing over answers and more about helping them find their own because that's where real growth sticks.

What about those of you who aren't having regular 1:1s or focusing on your team's development? What is your first move? Set up those regular 1:1 meetings and prioritize these. Do it today.

1:1s are dedicated time to connect human to human. They're not about checking boxes or running through task lists. They're a space to listen, ask real questions, clear roadblocks, and make sure your people feel seen, supported, and challenged. Done right, 1:1s build trust, sharpen focus, and create the kind of alignment that drives both performance and growth. It's where leadership shows up consistently, not just when there's a problem. It's also a time to listen to your team's needs in an empathetic and vulnerable way.

When you are ready to ramp up expectations, be transparent about when and why this is important to you, the team, and the organization. You are not doing anyone any favors by being complacent - expecting the same performance expectations year over year. This type of complacency is a symptom of invisibility. We already know that you cannot lead if you are invisible. Complacency is what happens when you get comfortable and stop stretching. It's that quiet slide from drive to drift when "good enough" starts to replace curiosity, urgency, and ownership. It doesn't always look like a problem, but it is one. Because once you stop questioning, stop reaching, and stop raising the bar, you stop growing. And teams don't move forward when everyone's standing still.

You can do everything right, hold the development discussions, offer coaching, provide feedback, and create opportunities but without trust, it won't matter. Trust is what makes those conversations meaningful and what turns coaching into growth. It's what allows feedback to be received as care instead of criticism. It's what makes your team believe that the opportunities you offer are truly in their best interest. At the heart of it all, trust is the difference between checking the box on leadership tasks and actually making an impact that lasts.

So, ask yourself, are your actions earning the kind of trust that makes real growth possible?

Chapter 9:
Appreciating Failure

In our earlier chapter, born to lead, we discussed how failure is a part of how teams learn and grow. While we aren't really sure if leaders are born, they are an essential part of a team's growth. Leaders create the space for success and failure because they know the team doesn't just learn from the wins—it learns even more from the misses. Failure is one of leadership's most underrated teachers. Failure is simply not getting the result you aimed for. It's feedback, not a final verdict, and it's often the very thing that points you toward the lesson you needed to learn.

It's uncomfortable, humbling, and often painful, but it's also necessary. Every time I failed, I discovered something I hadn't known about myself, my team, or the work I was leading. Sometimes those lessons were immediate. Other times, they revealed themselves in hindsight.

One of the most formative failures I experienced occurred while consulting for a company embarking on a digital transformation. I had been brought in to evaluate potential tools that could help automate and improve internal workflows. After months of research, pilot testing, and team collaboration, I presented a strategy that included introduction of new technologies. It was a robust, forward-thinking approach that could have revolutionized how the company operated.

However, their infrastructure couldn't support it. Their culture resisted it. For a while, I saw the decision as a rejection of my work. I felt I had failed.

But as I reflected, I realized the real failure wasn't the plan; it was the timing. My solution was technically sound, but emotionally and culturally misaligned.

Later, when I revisited the company a year after the initial proposal, I was surprised to find that two of the tools had been reintroduced, this time with excitement. The groundwork we laid had quietly nurtured readiness. It was a reminder that failure is often just a delay in success.

Another humbling moment came when I was asked to redesign a global onboarding experience. I poured my heart into it. The roadmap was sleek, strategic, and scalable. It had multi-tiered learning plans, tech integrations, and a phased rollout plan that would have made any HR leader proud. But to my excitement, I forgot the most crucial step: listening.

The business didn't want an overhaul. They needed simplification. They needed a few key compliance gaps filled. My proposal was too ambitious. It overwhelmed rather than inspired. And despite the hours invested, the project was tabled. That stung.

But here's what I took from that experience: Leadership isn't about being the hero. It's about focusing on the people, meeting them where they are, not dragging them where you think they should be.

- Failure isn't the opposite of success. It's part of it. Reflect on your mistakes; learn from them.
- A failed initiative can still plant the seeds of future success. Letting your team see you fail, or supporting your team when they fail will show your vulnerability and build trust.
- Listen more than you speak. You'll hear something and instantly want to jump in with your ideas. Pause. Listen fully. Sometimes, saying nothing means everything.

Supporting your team in moments of failure is so important. Here are some things you can reflect on about failure. Embrace it! Be that soft landing for your team.

- What did this teach me that success wouldn't have?
- Was this a failure, or just an unexpected step?
- How can I use this to move forward stronger?
- What will I do differently next time?

An effective way for your team to learn how to accept failure and learn from the lessons is to create experiments. An experiment doesn't have to be anything big, just pick something that you'd like to try out, say it's an experiment and get your team behind it. It may be successful, it may fail either way, you are coaching your team so that they can try things out without fear of judgement. By doing this, you are creating psychological safety that builds trust and provides support for your team to succeed.

Generative AI is all people talk about today. However, a few years ago, it was beginning to be popular, but no one knew it would have the impact it does today. In those early days of Generative AI becoming more available, I knew in my gut that this would help my team be more productive and, in turn, this would allow us the capacity to experiment with things that we didn't have time for. Not knowing if my team would be receptive, I announced, "Let's all use a Generative AI tool - any tool available to you, and let's see how many hours we can save in our day-to-day work". We kept it light; it's an experiment, let's see what happens. Because it was kept light, not something they were going to be evaluated on for their performance, but a trial to see if it would be helpful, this enabled the team to rally behind using it. Even those who were at first a little shy about it took to it quickly, realizing its power of bringing efficiencies. It was a successful experiment, and we did gain efficiency - enough to where the team felt that lift in their schedules. Now you'd think a leader would then say - okay, let's do more. Not so fast, that is the opposite of what we did. I shared that any gain in time, they can decide how they want to use that time they earned back. The time was substantial, but it was important to build trust by empowering the team to make this decision.

What if the experiment wasn't successful? We spend more time instead of less. We also found improved quality versus efficiency. It wasn't the result that was important; it was how we approached this as a team, how the team was empowered to have a safe space to try things out, learn, and apply without pressure or fear.

A leader who appreciates failure as much as success can make an enormous impact on their team, and even beyond. A leader who appreciates failure understands that progress is rarely a straight line. They know that every misstep carries a lesson, and that the real loss is when we fail to learn from it. They don't hide mistakes or brush past them; they pause, reflect, and invite the team to explore what happened and why.

This kind of leader sees failure as part of the process, not proof that someone isn't capable. They create an environment where people feel safe enough to take risks, speak up, and try bold ideas without fearing that one wrong turn will define them.

For them, failure is not the opposite of success, it's the soil where success grows. They recognize that some of the most innovative solutions, strongest skills, and deepest resilience come from lessons learned the hard way. They don't just say "it's okay to fail" they show it in how they respond, how they coach, and how they carry those lessons forward.

When a leader genuinely appreciates failure, they transform it from something to be feared into something that fuels growth. And that shift changes everything for the leader, for the team, and for what they can accomplish together.

Are you that leader? Will you be vulnerable, transparent, and visible to apply these lessons? Are you still afraid, teetering between invisibility and visibility?

Lesson 14: *Leaders aren't afraid to fail.*

I've failed many times in my career. I've failed more times than I've seen success. Each time I failed, I learned new things, what I want to do, and what I should not repeat. We are all human, and like most humans, we sometimes fall back into unhealthy habits. Failing is an essential part of leading. To be afraid to fail, or for your team to fail, simply means that leading might not be for you. Sounds harsh right? Without failure, learning never happens, which means your team does not develop.

So, how do you create an environment where you can learn from failure? Each leader will find their own way, but I'll share what worked for me, and it continues to evolve today:

- Trust your team. You hired your team, so let them do what they do. This is key to creating a safe environment where failure is allowed, trusting each other and having your team's back, even if it means owning a failure.

- Expect greatness. Develop your team to be continuous learners, thrive with change, and innovate often. Then, raise those expectations each year.
- Be a soft landing. Things may work out, but often they won't. Be calm, collected, and support your team through failures.
- Give feedback with empathy. The cooler you can be the more trust you build.
- Reflect on failure and learn how to turn it into success. This is the most important lesson I've learned. It's difficult, and you may want to point fingers or justify. Don't. Listen, listen, listen.
- Give your team the space to solve the problem. I'm a fixer, from years of fixing problems for people, and it's a hard habit to unlearn. Don't get me wrong, you need to support, but it should be through active listening and only asking questions to help them realize what they're missing on their own. One I use often is "Have you thought about _____?" or What do you think about _____?"

Lesson 15: *Learn to Appreciate Failure*

As I mentioned, failure is essential to being a leader. Think about Thomas Edison and how many times he failed before he perfected the light bulb. Or Steve Jobs, who could have given up after several failed attempts at creating the personal computer. We wouldn't have the iPhone today. Could you imagine life without it?

Nobody wants to fail. We all intend for things to go well, but then it hits you, this idea or product isn't going to land. This is where you either rise above it or let it defeat you. I've seen many great leaders deflated because, in their careers, they were always on top, until that day when failure defeated them. Your perception of failure is key. If failure means you are "less than," it defeats you. You begin to lose your confidence, and that makes it much harder to succeed the next time.

I remember a time when I was consulting, I presented recommendations for digital transformation, which included three technologies to implement based on the company's needs. Of the three, two were sidelined after the pilots, not because they weren't great ideas, but because the company wasn't ready for such a meaningful change. Some may have considered that a failure, but I didn't. The reason is that I celebrated the one improvement that did make an impact, where the company was ready for the change. Failure can be disguised in many ways, as in this scenario, where the company simply wasn't ready. It failed by not being implemented. Sometimes, failures aren't permanent. The best ideas that didn't take off may finally succeed, albeit in a different form. Take the Apple computer, how many times did Steve Jobs, and his co-creators work on the personal computer until they got it exactly right? That doesn't mean each failure proved the idea didn't have potential; it just wasn't ready to meet the need at the time. What I came to understand is that timing and focus matter just as much as the idea itself. You can have the right solution, but if the world or your organization isn't ready for it, it won't take root.

That's why one of the best pieces of advice from a former leader shared with me still stays with me today "don't boil the ocean". In other words, don't try to solve everything at once or take on more than can be done. Start where you can make the most meaningful impact. Prove the value in one area, then expand. It's a reminder that leadership isn't about spreading yourself thin it's about directing energy and resources where they'll matter most.

I was asked to propose an onboarding strategy and roadmap for a large global company. I was so excited and jumped at the opportunity. After much research and careful consideration, I made a proposal to the leader. It had three levels of options, and in my mind, it would have transformed how we attract onboard talent at the company. What I learned is that I didn't listen carefully to what the business needed. They didn't need a cutting-edge onboarding approach; they just needed me to simplify the process and address some audit requirements. This was a failure, a massive failure. Even though the recommendation was amazing, and I'd love to implement it sometime in the future, it didn't solve the problem. I was pretty defeated. I spent time and passion on something that didn't take flight. But after reflecting on it, the principles I learned from this one event have deeply impacted on how I work and how I lead. What I learned was that I needed to listen more and not be afraid to clarify what

I was asked to do. It's okay to come up with innovative ideas, but it must solve the problem at hand. A key principle of the teams I have led is "what problem are we solving?" By asking yourself and others these clarifying questions, I could have clarified the request and realized that the project, although smaller, could have been simplified and focused on the true root of the problem.

As a leader, you must create an environment where your team feels comfortable coming to you to ask questions, knowing that you are there to listen and be a safe place for them. Making mistakes shouldn't be punished, especially if you learn from them and grow. Each time a person makes a mistake, it brings them closer to the solution. A person's journey to the solution may be narrow, with twists and turns, or very direct. Every person is different, and a leader must be aware of this. One team member may not make mistakes often or at all. Does this make them a high performer? Is a person who makes many mistakes and learns from them less productive? It all depends on what they do with the information they learned and how they apply it toward their next opportunity to solve. solution.

That's why the way feedback is delivered matters just as much as the lesson itself. A simple correction can either build someone up or tear them down, depending on how it's given and received. What may seem like a small comment to a leader can leave an impression on the person hearing it.

Imagine having a leader who replied to an email correcting grammar. I didn't realize at the time, but it was her way to teach me how to improve my communication. The initial perspective was. Wow, this person had the gall to reply by red penning my words." Even when an intention may be there, it's important to think about how another will receive that feedback.

That experience taught me that feedback is more than pointing out mistakes—it's about creating an opportunity to learn. But here's the catch: not everyone learns the same way. Some people will take direct feedback and run with it, seeing it as a challenge to improve. Others may shut down if it feels harsh or overly critical. As leaders, it's not enough to simply give feedback; we have to understand the person receiving it, how they process information, and what helps them grow.

Understanding your team and how they learn is just as important as selecting the team members themselves. Giving a safe space to experiment and fail is essential to build trust and create a culture where failing isn't punished but celebrated. Yes, I said, "celebrate! Through failure, lessons are learned. The words in this book are a testament to many failures that led to impactful learnings.

Leaders will fail. If you are afraid to fail and take responsibility for these failures, you are not born to lead. Because here's the truth no one really is. Leadership isn't about being born with the right traits; it's about being willing to grow through the hard moments. Only by becoming visible, by owning both wins and failures, do you earn the trust to lead your team the way they deserve.

We talked about many things throughout this book. I had to go through the writings in this book, share my vulnerability to even author this book. All of these lessons will help you build your legacy as a leader. Will your legacy be "one to be remembered," or will your efforts go unnoticed, underutilized?

Chapter 10:
What Is Your Legacy as a Leader?

Legacy is the ripple you leave long after you've stepped away. It's the habits you've shaped, the trust you've built, and the example you've set that keep guiding others even when you're no longer in the room. Legacy isn't measured in awards or job titles, it's measured in the way people think, act, and lead differently because of how you showed up. What matters is not every action, but the impact you make.

What do people say about you when you're not in the room? That's your legacy.

It's not about what's on your résumé or LinkedIn profile; it's about how people remember how you made them feel. Did you inspire them? Challenge them? Help them grow? Or did you merely manage them?

I remember the first time someone told me I made a difference. It wasn't during a performance review or at a leadership seminar. It came in a handwritten note I received from a former team member: "I appreciate how you helped me build my self-esteem."

She was going through a rough time at work; it felt like everyone was against her. And when you already have low self-esteem, feeling like you fail at everything you do, that you can't do anything right, doesn't help; it just makes you perform worse.

Recently, a former team member shared on social media the award she had received. Being a proud "mamma," I commented that I was so proud of her. She replied with some kind words, saying the time spent on our team helped her realize her full potential.

Powerful words, and of course, I cried. To have an impact where, years later, people not only remember you but share words like that, it makes it all worth it.

It reminded me that leadership isn't about climbing the ladder. It's about lifting others. It's about planting seeds you may never see fully bloom. That's the kind of legacy I want to leave.

Legacy shows up in small moments, too. Like the time a former teammate sent me a thank you for being my leader or when a colleague reached out years later to say she still uses the feedback framework I taught her in her new role.

These moments are small in scope, but enormous in meaning.

Legacy also comes from how you lead through failure. I once had a team member who completely dropped the ball on a critical deliverable. It was a major mistake. Instead of reprimanding her, I sat her down and asked, "What happened? And how can I help you recover from this?" She burst into tears, not because she was afraid, but because she felt supported. She later told me it was the moment she realized what true leadership looked like.

- Legacy isn't built through grand gestures. It's built through daily choices.
- How you lead in someone's worst moment matters more than how you lead in their best.

Reflection Questions:

- What values do you want to be remembered for?
- Who have you helped progress?
- How do you want your team to describe you when you're no longer leading them?

Each week, reflect on one person you supported, mentored, challenged, or championed. Return to this reflection from time to time to keep yourself in the right mindset, focused on putting your team first.

Lesson 15: *Your legacy is not a future milestone.*

It's being written right now, in your actions, your words, and your presence.

Final Words

There are many stories and lessons woven through the pages of this book: moments of triumph, missteps that stung, and truths that took years to sink in. They are not polished fairy tales; they are real and imperfect, because leaders are, first, human beings. We are not flawless. We will stumble. We make the same mistake more than once, sometimes enough times to feel frustrated with ourselves, until finally the lesson takes root and shapes the way we lead.

The point isn't perfection, it's growth. A team member of mine reminded me more than a few times of "progress over perfection". This lesson was pivotal because it reminded me each time we take a step forward, no matter how small, we are making progress. Learn from the lessons your team will teach you. Offer yourself the grace to learn and do the same for your team. Every story here is a reminder that leadership is not about getting it all right, but about showing up, staying committed, and choosing to learn from your failures. If one of these lessons helps you avoid a misstep or recover from one, then these words have served their purpose.

A great leader wakes up thinking about their team before they think about themselves. They care about the team's well-being, their opportunities to grow, and the ambitions they carry in their hearts. A great leader doesn't just see the individuals; they see the potential of the whole. They put the needs of the team before their own comfort, status, or personal agenda. That doesn't mean they erase themselves, it means they lead from a place of service, knowing that when the team rises, everyone rises.

Leadership is not a title, a corner office, or a badge of authority. It's a daily choice to put people first, even when the decisions are tough, the hours are long, or the praise never comes. It's about listening when it is easier to talk, standing firm when it would be easier to give in, and caring deeply when it is safer to stay detached.

If you don't find joy in leading your team if their wins don't feel like your wins, if their growth doesn't excite you more than your own accolades, then it's worth asking yourself if leadership is where you genuinely want to be. Teams deserve leaders who are invested, present, and energized by their success. Anything less shortchanges the very people you've committed to serve.

So, learn from these lessons as well as reflect on your own. Share them openly, even when they reveal your flaws. And when you have the chance, use those lessons to help other leaders move forward with fewer scars and more clarity. Because leadership is not just about what you accomplish in your own tenure it's about what you leave behind in the leaders and teams who will carry the work forward. That's where your true legacy lives.

That's what these Leader Lessons are about, passing on the hard-earned truths so the path for the next leader is just a little clearer, a little kinder, and a little stronger.

This is where leading translates to impact.

www.ingramcontent.com/pod-product-compliance
Lightning Source LLC
Chambersburg PA
CBHW051331120626
46547CB00016B/2493